Insides Out!

by Lucille M. Kayes

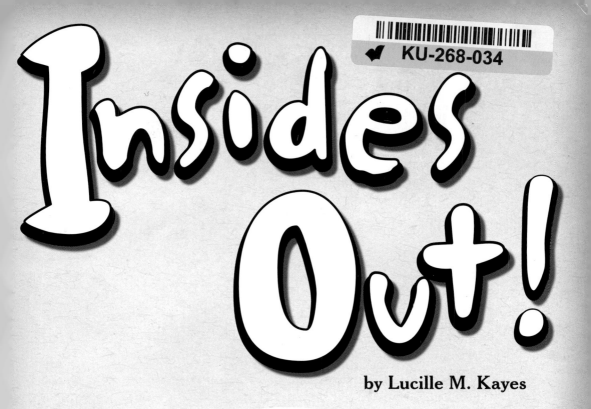

Welcome to the Lab!
To start exploring your
human body model right
away, turn to page 4!

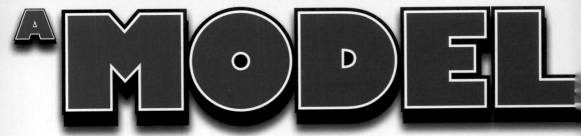

A MODEL

Insides Out!

Published by SmartLab®, an imprint of becker&mayer! All rights reserved.
SmartLab® is a registered trademark of becker&mayer! LLC
11120 NE 33rd Place, Suite 101, Bellevue, Washington.
Creative development by Jim Becker, Anna Johnson, and Aaron Tibbs

Edited by Nancy Waddell
Written by Lucille M. Kayes, MD
Art direction and design by Eddee Helms
Package design assistance by Wade Sherrard
Package illustration by Jeremy Friesen
Illustrated by Tyler Freidenrich and Ryan Hobson
SmartLab® character and product photography by Keith Megay
Additional photography by Grace. B. Lee and Jennifer A. Ramirez, ICANDI Studios
Product development by Drew Barr
Production management by Blake Mitchum and Beth Lenz
Project management by Beth Lenz
Photo research by Zena Chew
Facts checked by Karen Ball, ND
Special thanks to Kiah Helms, Patricia Riggin, Kate Hall,
Sydney Kamuda, Taylor Codomo, and Taylor Gwinn

Photo Credits:
Page 9: Photo of stomach lining ©David Musher / Photo Researchers, Inc.; Page 13: Photo of liver ©Anatomical Travelogue / Photo Researchers, Inc.; Page 19: Photo of heart ©Huberland / Photo Researchers, Inc.; Page 21: Photo of vocal cords ©Dr. James P. Thomas, taken with a flexible videoscope. Used with permission.; Page 23: Photo of right lung ©Southern Illinois University / Photo Researchers, Inc.
Every effort has been made to correctly attribute all the materials reproduced in this book. We will be happy to correct any errors in future editions.

Printed, manufactured, and assembled in China, September 2011 by Winner Printing & Packaging Ltd.

Insides Out! is part of the SmartLab® Squishy Human Body kit. Not to be sold separately.

The soft plastic organs of this product are a toy.
DO NOT EAT.
NONTOXIC

6 7 8 9 13 12 11

ISBN-10: 1-932855-78-5
ISBN-13: 978-1-932855-78-4

Distributed in the UK & ROI by:
Brainstorm, Ltd., Mill Lane, Gisburn
Lancashire BB7 4LN UK

SL06428-11793

120911

TABLE OF CONTENTS

LIFE

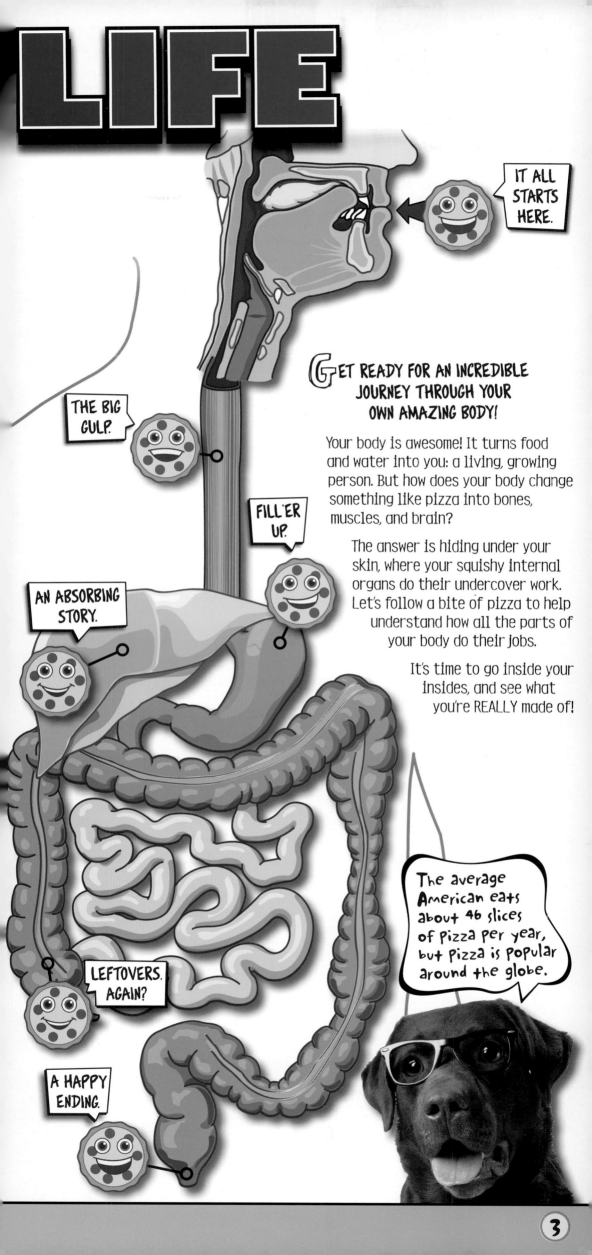

IT ALL STARTS HERE.

THE BIG GULP.

FILL 'ER UP.

AN ABSORBING STORY.

GET READY FOR AN INCREDIBLE JOURNEY THROUGH YOUR OWN AMAZING BODY!

Your body is awesome! It turns food and water into you: a living, growing person. But how does your body change something like pizza into bones, muscles, and brain?

The answer is hiding under your skin, where your squishy internal organs do their undercover work. Let's follow a bite of pizza to help understand how all the parts of your body do their jobs.

It's time to go inside your insides, and see what you're REALLY made of!

The average American eats about 46 slices of pizza per year, but pizza is popular around the globe.

LEFTOVERS. AGAIN?

A HAPPY ENDING.

GET ORGA

YOUR KIT INCLUDES A HUMAN BODY MODEL AND STAND WITH 9 REMOVABLE SQUISHY VITAL ORGANS, 12 PLASTIC BONES AND MUSCLES, FORCEPS, TWEEZERS, AND A BODY PARTS ORGAN-IZER TO KEEP TRACK OF ALL THE PARTS AS YOU EXPLORE.

THE VITALS

1 Lay your model on a flat surface. Hold down the model, and detach the rib cage (A). Place the rib cage on the ORGAN-IZER.

2 Lift the plastic sheet (B) while holding down the squishy organs. The parts are sticky, but be sure to keep them intact.

Now your model is ready. Time for the exploration of your life!

3 Use the ORGAN-IZER (C) to sort all the body parts as you explore. Match each body part to its outline. This way you can be sure you've removed the right part, and it will help when you put your model back together.

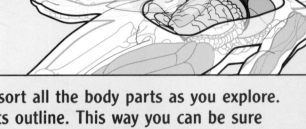

As you read through the book, use the forceps (D) and tweezers (E) to help you remove the squishy organs.

ORGAN·IZER

STOMACH
LUNGS
SKULL CAP
BRAIN
KIDNEYS
SKULL
SHOULDERS/SPINE/HIPS
FEMUR
TIBIA & FIBULA
LEG MUSCLE
FOOT

Use this chart to sort all of your model's body parts as you remove them. If you match them up as you go, it will be easier to put your model back together again. Explore away!

As you start pulling out the vital organs, you'll find that they are squishy and sticky. Be careful. You only want to remove one at a time. Have fun exploring the human body!

CELLULAR

CELLS ARE THE BUILDING BLOCKS OF THE ENTIRE BODY.

The human body isn't exactly solid, and it isn't exactly liquid. It's somewhere in between. That's because the body is made up of trillions of living cells.

Cells are like tiny water balloons: each one is a soft sac filled with liquid. If you glued a pile of water balloons together, it would be solid, but squishy—just like your body!

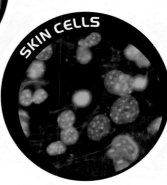

RED BLOOD CELLS

SKIN CELLS

TRY THIS!

FLEXIBILITY
FILL A BALLOON WITH WATER AND TIE IT SHUT. COMPARE ITS SQUISHINESS TO YOUR OWN MUSCLES.

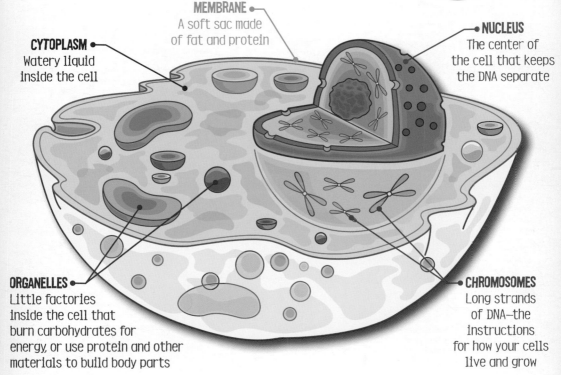

MEMBRANE
A soft sac made of fat and protein

CYTOPLASM
Watery liquid inside the cell

NUCLEUS
The center of the cell that keeps the DNA separate

ORGANELLES
Little factories inside the cell that burn carbohydrates for energy, or use protein and other materials to build body parts

CHROMOSOMES
Long strands of DNA—the instructions for how your cells live and grow

Q and A

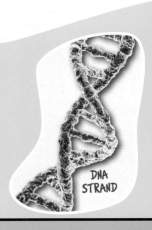

Q. WHAT DO THE LETTERS DNA STAND FOR?
A. It is short for deoxyribonucleic (dee-OX-ee-RY-bo-nu-CLAY-ik) acid.

Q. IF YOU STRETCHED OUT THE DNA FROM JUST ONE OF YOUR CELLS, HOW LONG WOULD IT BE?
A. It would be six feet long—as tall as an adult, but so thin you couldn't see it.

DNA STRAND

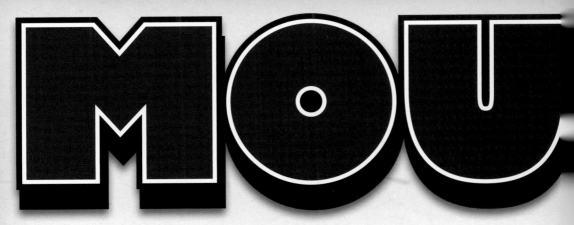

OPEN WIDE! ALL THE PARTS OF OUR MOUTH—LIPS, TEETH, AND TONGUE—WORK LIKE A FOOD PROCESSOR. LET'S FOLLOW A BITE OF PIZZA THROUGH YOUR BODY'S SYSTEM. THE JOURNEY STARTS WITH YOUR MOUTH.

THE VITALS

① A slice, or even a bite, of pizza is too big for your body to digest. Teeth bite and crush it into tiny pieces.

② Saliva (spit) has enzymes that start digesting the pizza before you even swallow. It breaks down the flour from the pizza crust into smaller sugar molecules.

③ When your mouth is finished, you swallow the chewed-up pizza. It goes down the esophagus to the stomach.

WHO'S HUNGRY? FOLLOW THE NUMBERS TO FOLLOW ME THROUGH YOUR VITAL ORGANS.

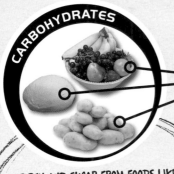

CARBOHYDRATES

ENERGY

STARCH AND SUGAR FROM FOODS LIKE PIZZA DOUGH, POTATOES, AND FRUIT ARE CALLED CARBOHYDRATES. THE BODY USES THEM TO MAKE ENERGY TO MOVE AND LIVE.

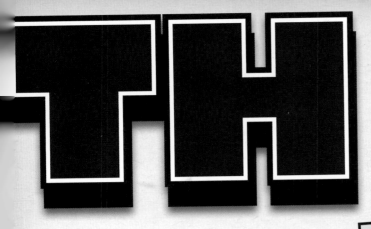
TH

TRY THIS!

"SEE" FOOD

WATCH YOURSELF EAT A CRACKER IN THE MIRROR. CHEW WITH YOUR MOUTH OPEN! WATCH YOUR TEETH AND TONGUE AT WORK. SEE HOW THE CRACKER GETS ALL WET AND SLIMY? DISGUSTING! WHY WOULD YOU WANT TO EAT THAT?

SENSATIONAL

TASTE AND SMELL WORK TOGETHER TO HELP US RECOGNIZE FOOD.

Your nose can recognize thousands of smells. Your tongue can recognize only five different tastes: **SWEET, SOUR, SALTY, BITTER, AND UMAMI (MEATY).**

When something tastes good, taste and smell are telling you it contains nutrients your body needs. That's why cereal tastes good, but the cereal box does not.

YOU MAKE ABOUT 4 CUPFULS OF SALIVA EVERY DAY.

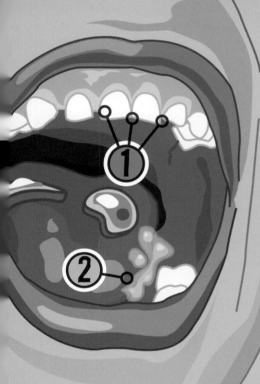

① ②

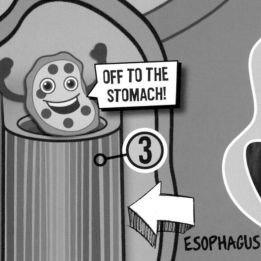

OFF TO THE STOMACH!

③

ESOPHAGUS

GROSS ALERT!

Your mouth is full of bacteria! Keep it clean by brushing your teeth, or you'll regret it.

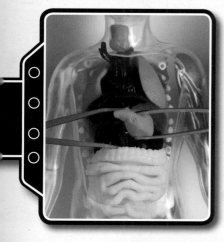

Your stomach is a muscular sac big enough to hold a meal. Even a whole pizza! It gets food ready for the body to use.

🐾 Your model's stomach is tan-colored. Spread your forceps on either side of it, touching the liver above it and the large intestine below it. Now, use the tweezers to pull out the stomach. Time to use your ORGAN-IZER so you can keep track of all your model's body parts.

THE VITALS

1. Muscles in the stomach wall squeeze food around to mix it.

2. Special cells along the sides of your stomach make a strong acid that breaks down the pizza even more. The acid dissolves the protein and the calcium from the cheese. (See Try This! below.)

3. Your stomach slowly squeezes out what's left of the pizza into the intestines for the next part of the adventure.

FEELING HUNGRY?

THAT'S WHAT HAPPENS WHEN YOUR STOMACH IS EMPTY. AS YOU EAT, IT STRETCHES, GIVING YOU THAT "FULL" FEELING.

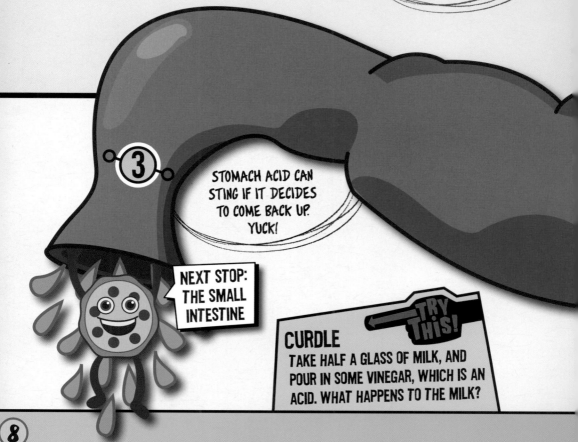

③ STOMACH ACID CAN STING IF IT DECIDES TO COME BACK UP. YUCK!

NEXT STOP: THE SMALL INTESTINE

TRY THIS!

CURDLE
TAKE HALF A GLASS OF MILK, AND POUR IN SOME VINEGAR, WHICH IS AN ACID. WHAT HAPPENS TO THE MILK?

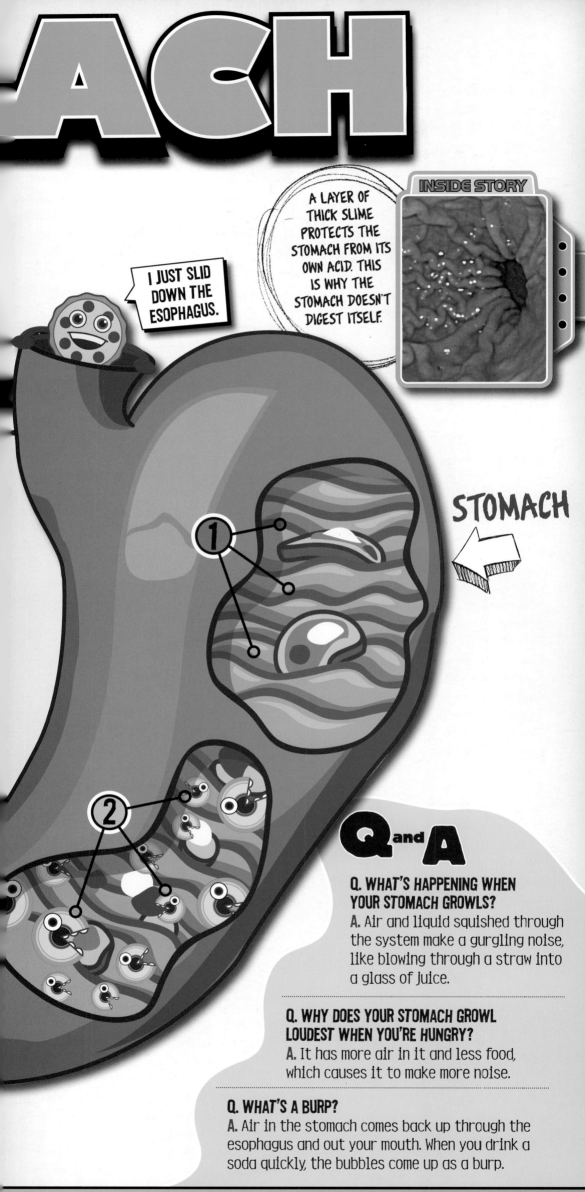

ACH

A LAYER OF THICK SLIME PROTECTS THE STOMACH FROM ITS OWN ACID. THIS IS WHY THE STOMACH DOESN'T DIGEST ITSELF.

INSIDE STORY

I JUST SLID DOWN THE ESOPHAGUS.

STOMACH

Q and A

Q. WHAT'S HAPPENING WHEN YOUR STOMACH GROWLS?
A. Air and liquid squished through the system make a gurgling noise, like blowing through a straw into a glass of juice.

Q. WHY DOES YOUR STOMACH GROWL LOUDEST WHEN YOU'RE HUNGRY?
A. It has more air in it and less food, which causes it to make more noise.

Q. WHAT'S A BURP?
A. Air in the stomach comes back up through the esophagus and out your mouth. When you drink a soda quickly, the bubbles come up as a burp.

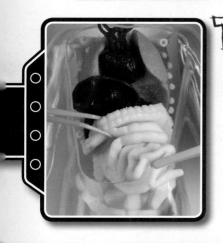

TOGETHER, YOUR SMALL AND LARGE INTESTINES ARE ONE LONG, SQUISHY TUBE. ONE END IS CONNECTED TO THE STOMACH, AND THE OTHER END IS CONNECTED TO, WELL, YOUR "OTHER END."

🐾 USING YOUR TWEEZERS, PULL ON THE SMALL INTESTINE PART OF THIS PIECE. SEE HOW LONG IT IS? IT'S CONNECTED TO THE LARGE INTESTINE THAT SURROUNDS IT. USE YOUR FORCEPS TO REMOVE THIS ENTIRE PIECE.

THE VITALS

① The small intestine adds substances to the stomach acid. This makes it harmless to the delicate lining of the small intestine.

② Enzymes from the small intestine breaks down all the nutrients into the tiniest molecules.

③ Fuzzy hair-like cells along the inside of the small intestine, called villi (VIL-eye), absorb the nutrients and pass them along into your blood: protein from the cheese, sugar from the crust, vitamins from the sauce, and fat from the oil.

④ Things like the tough fiber from the pizza's tomatoes gets squirted into your large intestine. It absorbs much of the leftover water, leaving thick, brown POOP!

⑤ Bacteria in your large intestine feast on your poop.

The **LARGE** intestine is about the length of an ironing board—much shorter than the **SMALL** intestine, which is about 23 feet long. It is called "large" because it's wider and thicker.

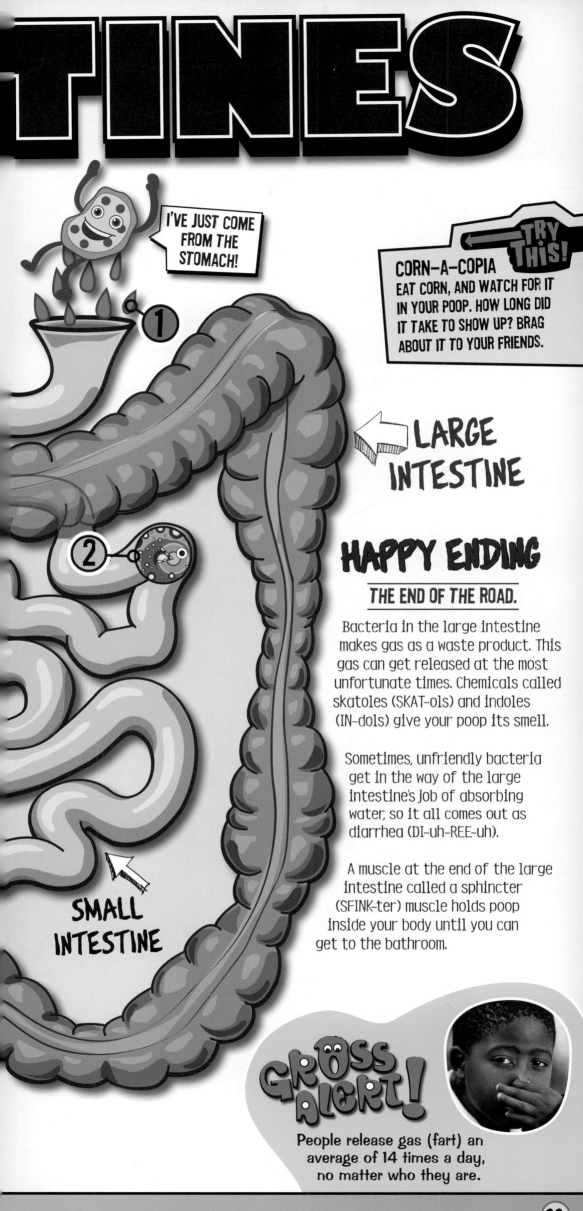

I'VE JUST COME FROM THE STOMACH!

TRY THIS!

CORN-A-COPIA
EAT CORN, AND WATCH FOR IT IN YOUR POOP. HOW LONG DID IT TAKE TO SHOW UP? BRAG ABOUT IT TO YOUR FRIENDS.

1

2

LARGE INTESTINE

SMALL INTESTINE

HAPPY ENDING

THE END OF THE ROAD.

Bacteria in the large intestine makes gas as a waste product. This gas can get released at the most unfortunate times. Chemicals called skatoles (SKAT-ols) and indoles (IN-dols) give your poop its smell.

Sometimes, unfriendly bacteria get in the way of the large intestine's job of absorbing water, so it all comes out as diarrhea (DI-uh-REE-uh).

A muscle at the end of the large intestine called a sphincter (SFINK-ter) muscle holds poop inside your body until you can get to the bathroom.

GROSS ALERT!

People release gas (fart) an average of 14 times a day, no matter who they are.

LIVER

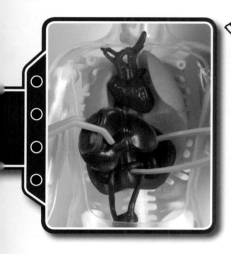

You can't live without your liver! It's your largest internal organ and acts as the body's security guard.

🐾 Your model's liver is brown. The flat, red piece behind the liver is the diaphragm. It may stick to the liver, so hold the diaphragm in place with the tweezers, and pull out the liver with your forceps.

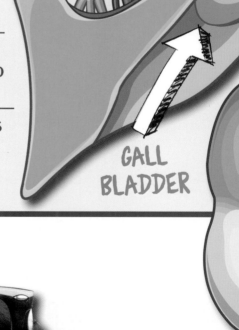

FINALLY, OFF TO THE HEART!

④

TO THE HEART

THE VITALS

① All the blood from your intestines goes to your liver first. (The flow of blood starts at the bottom of this illustration.)

② Nutrients from the pizza go through your liver to get processed. The liver decides whether to store them or let them through, depending on what your body needs.

③ The liver keeps poisons, such as food preservatives, from going to the rest of the body.

④ When your liver is done, it sends the blood to your heart, so the nutrients from the pizza can be sent all over your body.

GALL BLADDER

The liver is the only human organ that can regrow if injured.

THE LIVER IS DENSE WITH LOTS OF BLOOD FLOWING THROUGH IT.

LIVER

③

② STOMACH

THAT'S BILE

THE GALL BLADDER ROCKS!

Has your vomit ever been green? That's because of the bile. The liver makes bile, which helps digest fat. It is stored in the gall bladder until needed, then squirted into the small intestine.

Substances in bile can sometimes form hard lumps called gallstones. Most are smaller than a pea. But the biggest gallstone on record weighed 14 pounds!

14 POUND GALLSTONE

14 POUND BOWLING BALL

FAT

① TO THE LIVER

SMALL INTESTINE

I WAS JUST IN THE INTESTINES!

TRY THIS!

LET THEM EAT LIVER!
BECAUSE IT STORES NUTRIENTS, AN ANIMAL'S LIVER IS ONE OF THE MOST NUTRITIOUS MEATS YOU CAN EAT. MANY STORES SELL LIVERWURST IN THE LUNCHMEAT SECTION. TRY A LIVERWURST SANDWICH!

KIDNEYS

You have a pair of kidneys that are the body's plumbing system. They are shaped like large kidney beans.

🐾 Now that the intestines are out of the way, you can see the kidneys and bladder lying on top of the diaphragm. Use your tweezers to remove them. You may need to hold the sticky diaphragm in place again.

THE VITALS

KIDNEY →

1. Blood flows into the kidneys for filtering. They can filter all of your blood as much as 400 times per day.

2. The blood is filtered through millions of tiny loops called nephrons (NEF-rons).

3. Ureters are tubes that carry urine (pee) from your kidneys to your bladder.

4. Your bladder stores urine until a convenient time for you to, well, pee. When it's about half full, you start to feel the urge.

5. You control a little muscle called a sphincter (SFINK-ter) at the bottom of the bladder to let it out when you're ready.

6. The urethra (yu-REE-thra) carries the urine out of the body. The bladder relaxes, and you feel relief.

YOU CAN LIVE WITH ONLY ONE KIDNEY!

Drink plenty of water so your kidneys can do their job. They filter four cups of blood every minute!

GROSS ALERT!

Some people believe drinking pee keeps you healthy.

AND BLADDER

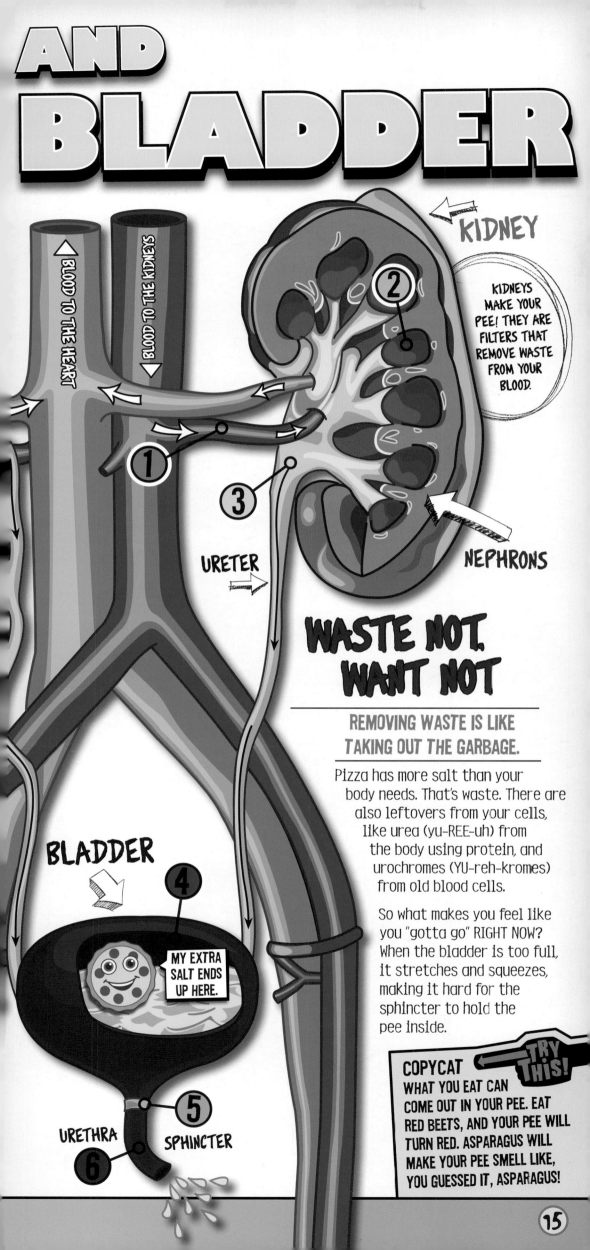

BLOOD TO THE HEART

BLOOD TO THE KIDNEYS

KIDNEY

KIDNEYS MAKE YOUR PEE! THEY ARE FILTERS THAT REMOVE WASTE FROM YOUR BLOOD.

① ② ③

NEPHRONS

URETER

WASTE NOT, WANT NOT

REMOVING WASTE IS LIKE TAKING OUT THE GARBAGE.

Pizza has more salt than your body needs. That's waste. There are also leftovers from your cells, like urea (yu-REE-uh) from the body using protein, and urochromes (YU-reh-kromes) from old blood cells.

So what makes you feel like you "gotta go" RIGHT NOW? When the bladder is too full, it stretches and squeezes, making it hard for the sphincter to hold the pee inside.

BLADDER

④ MY EXTRA SALT ENDS UP HERE.

⑤

URETHRA ⑥ **SPHINCTER**

COPYCAT TRY THIS!
WHAT YOU EAT CAN COME OUT IN YOUR PEE. EAT RED BEETS, AND YOUR PEE WILL TURN RED. ASPARAGUS WILL MAKE YOUR PEE SMELL LIKE, YOU GUESSED IT, ASPARAGUS!

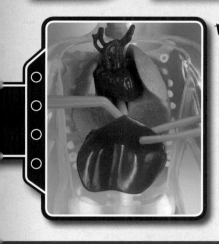

The DIAPHRAGM IS A THIN, FLAT MUSCLE LOCATED BELOW YOUR LUNGS IN THE RIB CAGE. IT IS YOUR MOST IMPORTANT BREATHING MUSCLE.

🐾 USE YOUR TWEEZERS TO REMOVE THE RED, CUP-SHAPED DIAPHRAGM. YOU MAY NEED TO HOLD DOWN THE LUNGS WITH YOUR FORCEPS. KEEP USING YOUR ORGAN-IZER!

TRACHEA ➡

THE VITALS

① The diaphragm (DIE uh fram) is a muscle. Its movement draws air into your lungs. First, it tightens and gets flat.

② The space in the rib cage is bigger and draws in air. This is you breathing in.

③ The diaphragm relaxes, and curves up under the ribs.

④ Air is let out of the lungs. This is you breathing out.

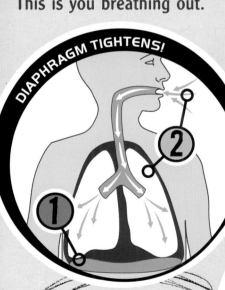

DIAPHRAGM TIGHTENS!

WATCH SOMEONE'S CHEST WHEN THEY'RE BREATHING HARD. WHEN YOU ARE BREATHING REALLY FAST YOUR RIB MUSCLES HELP TO LIFT THE RIBS UP AND DRAW MORE AIR INTO YOUR LUNGS.

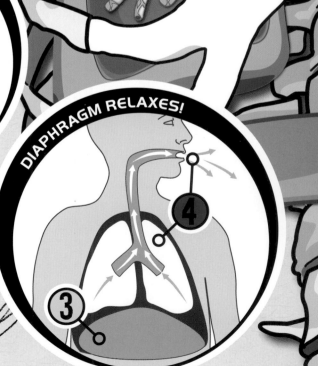

DIAPHRAGM RELAXES!

Q and A

Q. WHAT ARE HICCUPS?
A. They are spasms (sudden movements) of the diaphragm. There are lots of ways people try to stop them, like holding their breath and counting to 10. But none of these tricks really work.

Q. WHY DO YOU GET A PAIN IN YOUR SIDE WHEN YOU RUN TOO FAR?
A. That pain in your side is a pain in the diaphragm! It comes from not getting enough oxygen. It doesn't happen as much when you exercise regularly.

RIB CAGE

LUNG

BREATHLESS

SO WHAT DOES THE DIAPHRAGM HAVE TO DO WITH THE PIZZA?

Plenty! The diaphragm is a muscle, and muscles are made of protein. Protein from the pizza's cheese will make your diaphragm strong. It takes energy to move muscles, and energy comes from the carbohydrates in the pizza crust.

The record for the longest hiccups is 69 years. A man started hiccuping in 1922 in his late 20s. His hiccuping finally stopped in 1990, one year before he died.

I MAKE THE DIAPHRAGM STRONG!

DIAPHRAGM

HEART

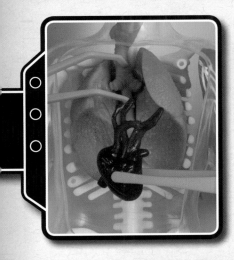

LOVE YOUR HEART! IT'S A STRONG, THICK MUSCLE FOR PUMPING BLOOD. BLOOD FLOWS IN TUBES ALL AROUND THE BODY, LIKE A GIANT WATER SLIDE!

🐾 USE YOUR TWEEZERS TO TAKE ANOTHER LITTLE PIECE OUT—THE HEART! IT MAY STICK TO YOUR ESOPHAGUS/TRACHEA SO USE YOUR FORCEPS TO HOLD THIS PIECE IN PLACE.

THE VITALS

① Nutrients from the liver flow to the heart. (The action starts at the bottom of this illustration.)

② The right side of the heart pumps blood through the lungs to pick up oxygen. Now the blood has both food and oxygen and is ready for the body to use!

③ The blood flows back to the heart.

④ The left side of the heart is stronger because it needs more power to pump blood way out to your fingers and toes. Whoosh! Now the pizza is headed out all over your body!

⑤ Arteries carry blood and oxygen to the body. Vitamin C from the tomato sauce keeps arteries and veins healthy.

⑥ Veins carry used blood back to the heart to get more oxygen from the lungs.

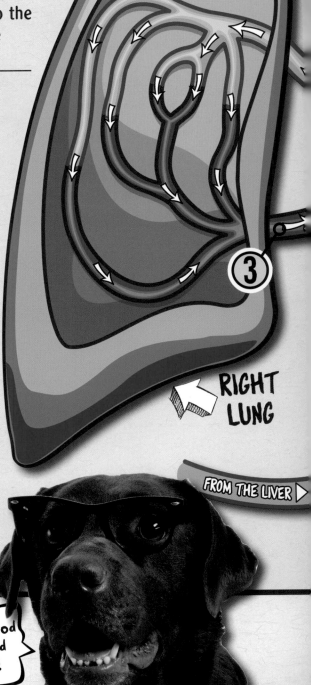

RIGHT LUNG

FROM THE LIVER ▶

Blue equals used blood and red equals blood with fresh oxygen!

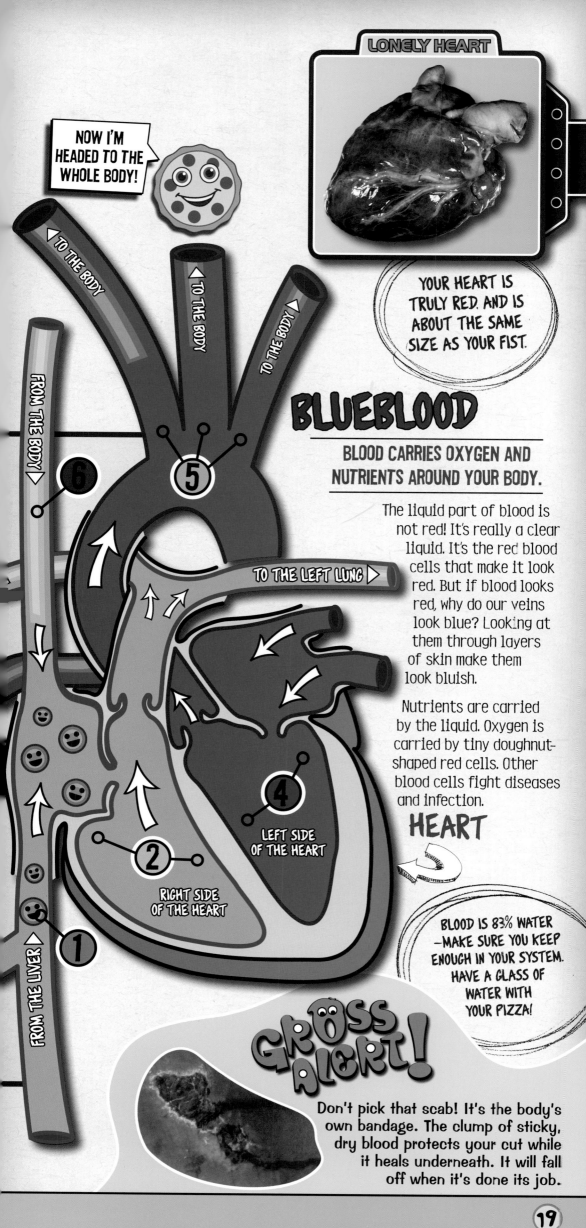

NOW I'M HEADED TO THE WHOLE BODY!

YOUR HEART IS TRULY RED. AND IS ABOUT THE SAME SIZE AS YOUR FIST.

TO THE BODY

TO THE BODY

TO THE BODY

FROM THE BODY

⑥

⑤

TO THE LEFT LUNG ▷

④

LEFT SIDE OF THE HEART

②

RIGHT SIDE OF THE HEART

①

FROM THE LIVER ▷

BLUEBLOOD

BLOOD CARRIES OXYGEN AND NUTRIENTS AROUND YOUR BODY.

The liquid part of blood is not red! It's really a clear liquid. It's the red blood cells that make it look red. But if blood looks red, why do our veins look blue? Looking at them through layers of skin make them look bluish.

Nutrients are carried by the liquid. Oxygen is carried by tiny doughnut-shaped red cells. Other blood cells fight diseases and infection.

HEART

BLOOD IS 83% WATER —MAKE SURE YOU KEEP ENOUGH IN YOUR SYSTEM. HAVE A GLASS OF WATER WITH YOUR PIZZA!

GROSS ALERT!

Don't pick that scab! It's the body's own bandage. The clump of sticky, dry blood protects your cut while it heals underneath. It will fall off when it's done its job.

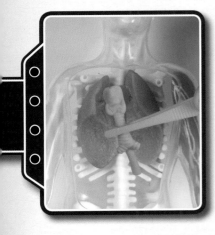

Your MOUTH IS USED FOR BREATHING AND EATING. SO HOW DO AIR AND FOOD GET TO THE RIGHT PLACES? YOUR THROAT STARTS OUT AS ONE TUBE AND SPLITS INTO TWO.

🐾 YOUR MODEL'S ESOPHAGUS AND TRACHEA ARE ATTACHED AS ONE THIN TAN-COLORED PIECE THAT LIES BETWEEN THE LUNGS. USE YOUR TWEEZERS TO GRAB THIS COMBINATION ORGAN.

THE VITALS

① The mouth and tongue help you chew and swallow.

② When you swallow, the epiglottis closes and covers the trachea, sometimes called the windpipe. The epiglottis is a piece of cartilage that stays open for breathing but closes off the trachea when you swallow. This trap door keeps food from going down the wrong tube.

③ Muscles push food and liquid down the esophagus to the stomach.

④ After you swallow, the tongue relaxes, and the epiglottis opens so you can breathe again.

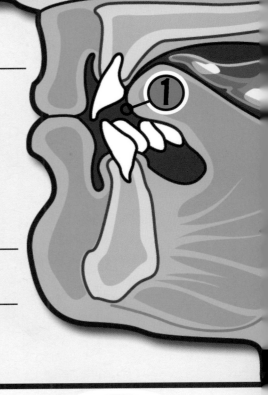

You can't breathe and swallow at the same time, but babies can.

EPIGLOTTIS OPENED

GOOD VIBRATIONS

VOCAL CORDS MAKE SOUND TO TALK AND TO SING.

The voice box, or larynx, is located at the top of the trachea. Stretched along the sides are two little strands—your vocal cords. When you tighten them and breathe out, the air passes between the vocal cords, making them vibrate just like guitar strings.

HERE I AM, ALL CHEWED UP.

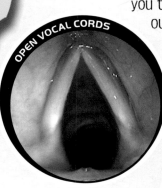

OPEN VOCAL CORDS

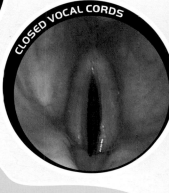

CLOSED VOCAL CORDS

Q and A

Q. WHY DO BOYS' VOICES CHANGE?
A. The voice box goes through a growth spurt, and the vocal cords get thicker and longer, creating a deeper sound. Girls' voice boxes don't grow as much.

Q. WHAT HAPPENS WHEN SOMETHING "GOES DOWN THE WRONG WAY"?
A. If food or drink trickles down when the epiglottis is open, it gets into the trachea, and your body coughs to get it out.

Q. WHAT IS A COUGH?
A. A cough is a powerful blast of air to clear something out of your trachea.

Q. WHAT IS A SNEEZE?
A. A sneeze is like a cough, but directed out your nose to clear it. Can you sneeze with your eyes open? Most people can't.

(2)
EPIGLOTTIS CLOSED

(3)

VOCAL CORDS

AIR

ESOPHAGUS

TRACHEA

LUNGS

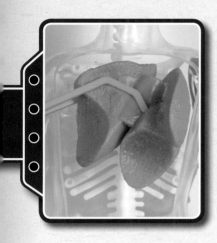

Like the kidneys, the lungs come in a pair. They bring oxygen into the body. This helps burn carbohydrates from the pizza to make energy for living.

🐾 It's hard to miss the double-part lungs. Use your forceps to remove this squishy organ from your model. There's a second plastic sheet underneath the lungs. Remove and dispose of it.

LUNG

THE VITALS

1. Oxygen comes from the air. The diaphragm contracts and draws air through the trachea and into the lungs.

2. The air ends up in tiny sacs containing alveoli (al-VEE-o-lie).

   The heart pumps blood to your lungs.

3. Blood flows closely around the sacs.

4. Oxygen passes through the sac wall into the blood. Oxygen is picked up by the red blood cells.

5. Blood goes back to the heart. The heart pumps the oxygen-rich blood all over your body.

MY CARBS ARE BURNING!

ALVEOLAR SACS

DIAPHRAGM

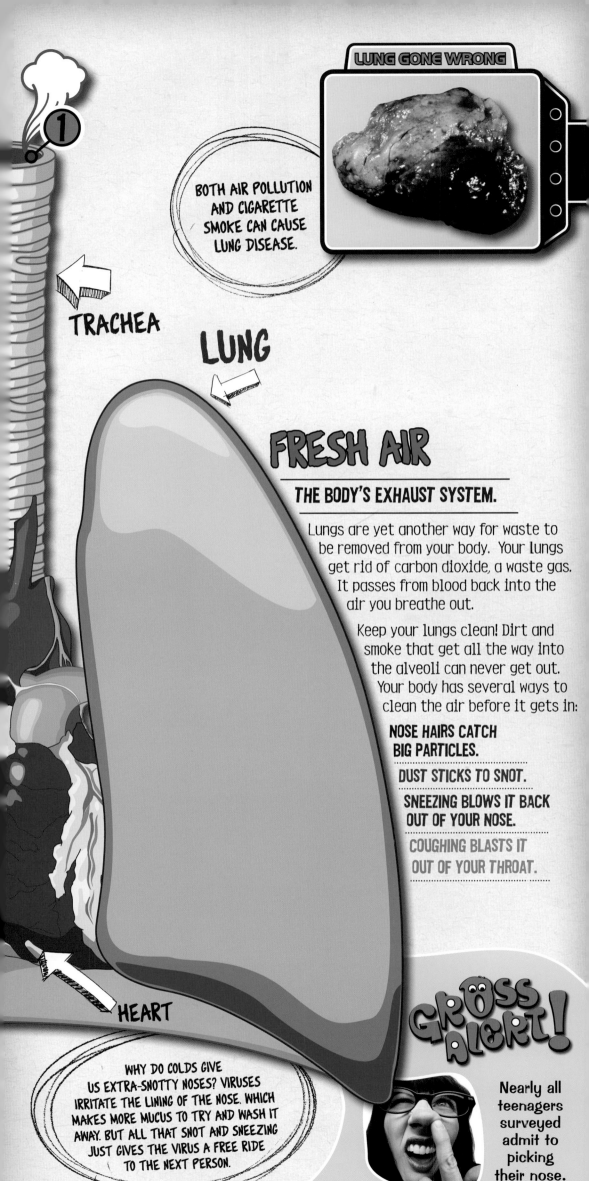

①

BOTH AIR POLLUTION AND CIGARETTE SMOKE CAN CAUSE LUNG DISEASE.

TRACHEA

LUNG

FRESH AIR

THE BODY'S EXHAUST SYSTEM.

Lungs are yet another way for waste to be removed from your body. Your lungs get rid of carbon dioxide, a waste gas. It passes from blood back into the air you breathe out.

Keep your lungs clean! Dirt and smoke that get all the way into the alveoli can never get out. Your body has several ways to clean the air before it gets in:

NOSE HAIRS CATCH BIG PARTICLES.

DUST STICKS TO SNOT.

SNEEZING BLOWS IT BACK OUT OF YOUR NOSE.

COUGHING BLASTS IT OUT OF YOUR THROAT.

HEART

GROSS ALERT!

WHY DO COLDS GIVE US EXTRA-SNOTTY NOSES? VIRUSES IRRITATE THE LINING OF THE NOSE, WHICH MAKES MORE MUCUS TO TRY AND WASH IT AWAY. BUT ALL THAT SNOT AND SNEEZING JUST GIVES THE VIRUS A FREE RIDE TO THE NEXT PERSON.

Nearly all teenagers surveyed admit to picking their nose.

SKIN

Your skin keeps all your body parts intact. It adapts to sun and temperature. And it changes with age and body chemistry.

🐾 THE SKIN ON YOUR MODEL IS CLEAR. REMOVE THE TOP LAYER OF SKIN BY GENTLY PRESSING ON THE TOP OF THE HEAD AND CAREFULLY LIFTING AND UNSNAPPING THE FRONT PART OF THE MODEL. SET THE SKIN TO THE SIDE OF YOUR ORGAN-IZER.

COLORFUL

DIFFERENT SKIN COLORS ARE JUST DIFFERENT AMOUNTS OF MELANIN.

THE VITALS

① With body changes, skin gets oilier and sweatier. Clogged glands get infected, causing zits.

② Melanin is a brown color in our skin that protects us from the sun. In some people's skin, melanin only forms in little spots, called freckles.

③ Dandruff is flakes of dead skin and oil that get stuck in our hair.

④ Sweat doesn't smell until bacteria grow in it. Adult armpit sweat is thicker, and bacteria grow better in it.

⑤ Each hair has a little muscle attached to it. When you are cold or scared, the muscle contracts and makes bumps called goosebumps.

Skin is your largest vital organ. An adult's skin weighs about 6 pounds. That's more than 5 basketballs!

④

⑤

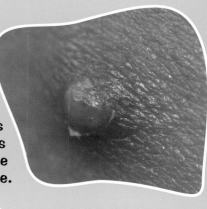

COMPLEXION

SKIN IS MORE COMPLICATED THAN IT LOOKS.

Skin is covered with hair, except for the palms of your hands and the soles of your feet. The outer layer of skin is dead cells, which flake off all the time. But underneath is alive! New cells are always growing.

Blood flows under your skin, bringing **NUTRIENTS** from the pizza: **PROTEIN** and **CARBOHYDRATES** for growth, and **VITAMINS** to help you stay healthy.

I HELP YOU MAKE A WHOLE NEW SKIN EVERY MONTH!

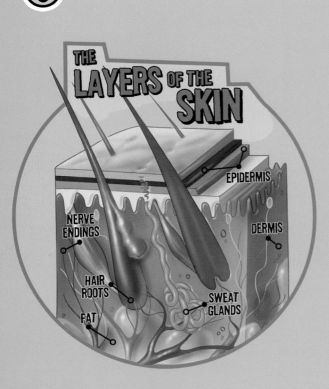

THE LAYERS OF THE SKIN

EPIDERMIS

NERVE ENDINGS

DERMIS

HAIR ROOTS

SWEAT GLANDS

FAT

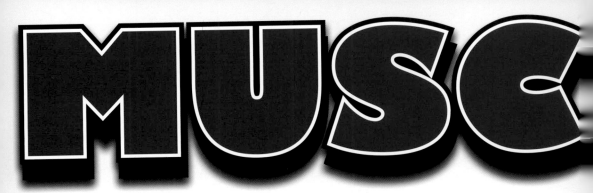

MUSC

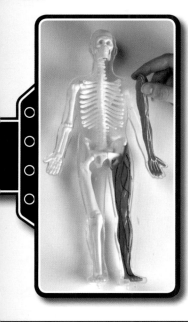

Muscles connect your bones together so they can move. The pizza is really needed here because your muscles use lots of protein to build strength, carbohydrates for energy, and vitamins to stay healthy.

🐾 Your model's muscles are kept in place with plastic plugs. Carefully pull out the arm muscle and the leg muscle with your fingers. Your model's arm has nerves shown in white. Your model's leg has arteries and veins shown in red and blue.

MUSCLE MAN

RESTING MUSCLES ARE SOFT AND SQUISHY. WORKING MUSCLES ARE STIFF AND HELP YOU LEAP TALL BUILDINGS IN A SINGLE BOUND.

THE VITALS

① Your body has three types of muscles: SKELETAL (voluntary), CARDIAC (involuntary), and SMOOTH (involuntary). Skeletal muscles are called voluntary because they move when you tell them to move: nerves carry messages from the brain, telling the muscles what to do. When nerves stop sending messages, the muscle can relax.

② The muscles in your arms control your hands and fingers. These are also skeletal muscles. They are strong enough for push-ups and delicate enough for writing.

③ The cardiac muscle is your heart muscle. It is called an involuntary muscle. You don't have to think about it—it's always working.

④ Smooth muscles are mostly in your guts. They are involuntary so they do their job—breathing air into your lungs or grinding up food in your stomach—without you having to think about it.

Your smallest muscle is in your ear and is called the stapedius. It controls your body's smallest bone, the stirrup bone.

⑤ Leg muscles are big and strong. You use them for walking, running, and jumping. But you sit on the biggest muscle of them all—your gluteus maximus.

BONES

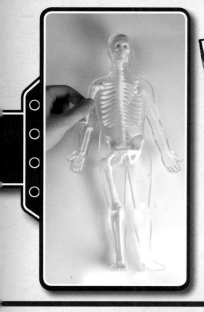

WITHOUT BONES YOU'D BE A BLOB! BONES ARE LIVING, GROWING BODY PARTS THAT NEED BLOOD TO BRING IN OXYGEN AND NUTRIENTS.

🐾 YOUR MODEL'S BONES ARE HELD IN PLACE WITH PLASTIC PLUGS. ITS EASY TO MIX THEM UP. USING YOUR FINGERS, CAREFULLY PULL OUT EACH BONE IN THIS ORDER:

- FIRST THE ARM—HAND, RADIUS AND ULNA, HUMERUS.
- THEN THE LEG—FOOT, TIBIA AND FIBULA, FEMUR.
- FINALLY THE BODY—THE SHOULDER/SPINE/HIP PIECE.

TO-MARROW

Many bones are hollow, with blood flowing on the inside. In fact, bones produce your blood cells inside the center part, called the marrow.

VEINS & ARTERIES

COMPACT BONE

MARROW CAVITY

SPONGY BONE

Tiny, squishy bone cells surround themselves with calcium, which makes bones hard and strong. **YOU HAVE 206 BONES IN YOUR BODY.** That's a lot of calcium!

CHEESE FROM THE PIZZA IS A GOOD SOURCE OF CALCIUM. BONES NEED ALL KINDS OF OTHER NUTRIENTS AND VITAMINS. TOO!

WORK-IN-PROGRESS

Kids' bones are special because they are still growing. They are hard, but not like rocks. Parts of them are made of cartilage, which feels rubbery, like your ears and your nose. The ends, where the joints come together, are also covered in cartilage.

KNEE X-RAY

CARTILAGE

KNEE BONE

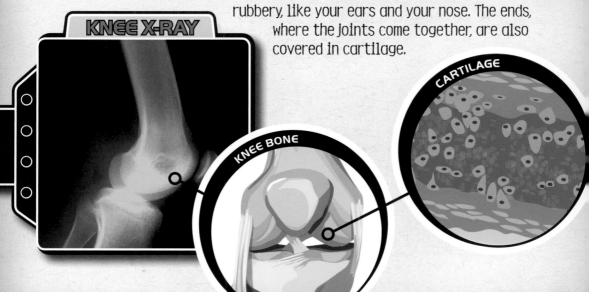

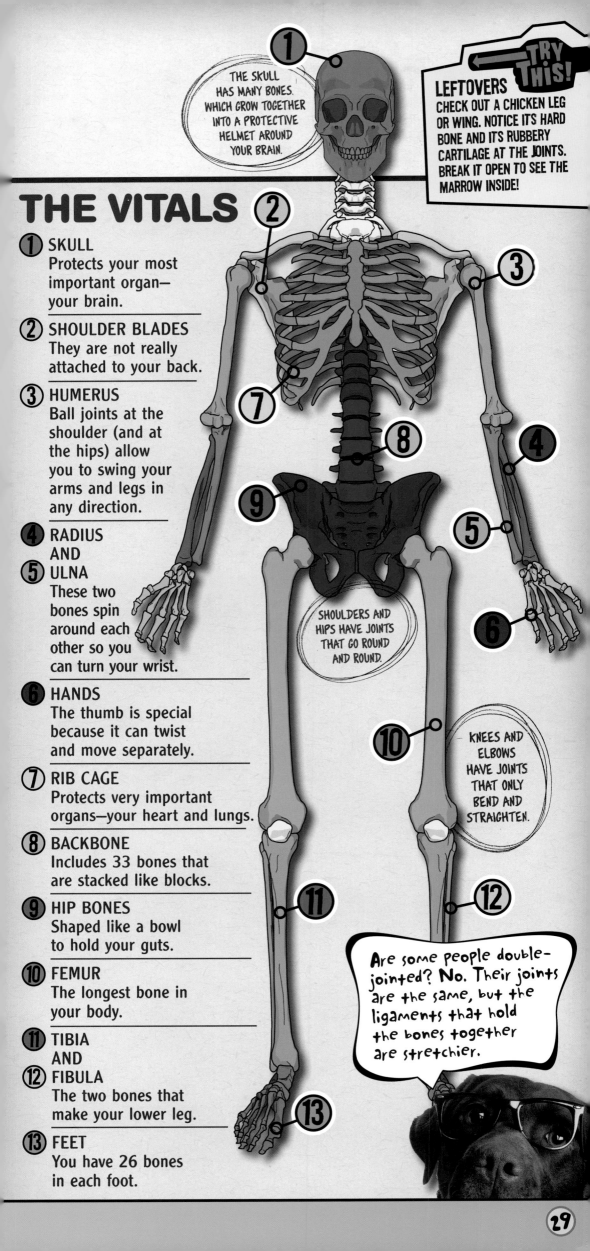

THE SKULL HAS MANY BONES. WHICH GROW TOGETHER INTO A PROTECTIVE HELMET AROUND YOUR BRAIN.

TRY THIS!

LEFTOVERS
CHECK OUT A CHICKEN LEG OR WING. NOTICE ITS HARD BONE AND ITS RUBBERY CARTILAGE AT THE JOINTS. BREAK IT OPEN TO SEE THE MARROW INSIDE!

THE VITALS

① SKULL
Protects your most important organ—your brain.

② SHOULDER BLADES
They are not really attached to your back.

③ HUMERUS
Ball joints at the shoulder (and at the hips) allow you to swing your arms and legs in any direction.

④ RADIUS AND
⑤ ULNA
These two bones spin around each other so you can turn your wrist.

⑥ HANDS
The thumb is special because it can twist and move separately.

⑦ RIB CAGE
Protects very important organs—your heart and lungs.

⑧ BACKBONE
Includes 33 bones that are stacked like blocks.

⑨ HIP BONES
Shaped like a bowl to hold your guts.

⑩ FEMUR
The longest bone in your body.

⑪ TIBIA AND
⑫ FIBULA
The two bones that make your lower leg.

⑬ FEET
You have 26 bones in each foot.

SHOULDERS AND HIPS HAVE JOINTS THAT GO ROUND AND ROUND.

KNEES AND ELBOWS HAVE JOINTS THAT ONLY BEND AND STRAIGHTEN.

Are some people double-jointed? No. Their joints are the same, but the ligaments that hold the bones together are stretchier.

BRAIN

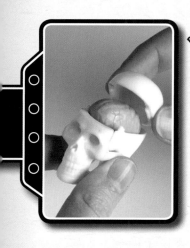

Your brain is the softest, squishiest body part of all! An adult brain is like jello; a kid's brain is thicker than pudding, but not much.

🐾 REMOVE THE SKULL FROM YOUR MODEL, USING YOUR FINGERS. TAKE OFF THE SKULL CAP AND USE THE TWEEZERS TO REMOVE THE BRAIN.

THE VITALS

① The brain decides it wants to touch something, like another piece of pizza or a glass of water.

② It sends messages down the nerves to the arm and hand, telling muscles to reach out the hand.

③ Special cells in the skin sense pain, heat, cold, or touch.

④ Messages about what you are touching travel back to the brain.

⑤ The brain recognizes what you feel.

RIGHT NOW, YOUR BRAIN IS THINKING ABOUT YOUR BRAIN!